PRANKS, TRICKS, AND PRACTICAL JOKES

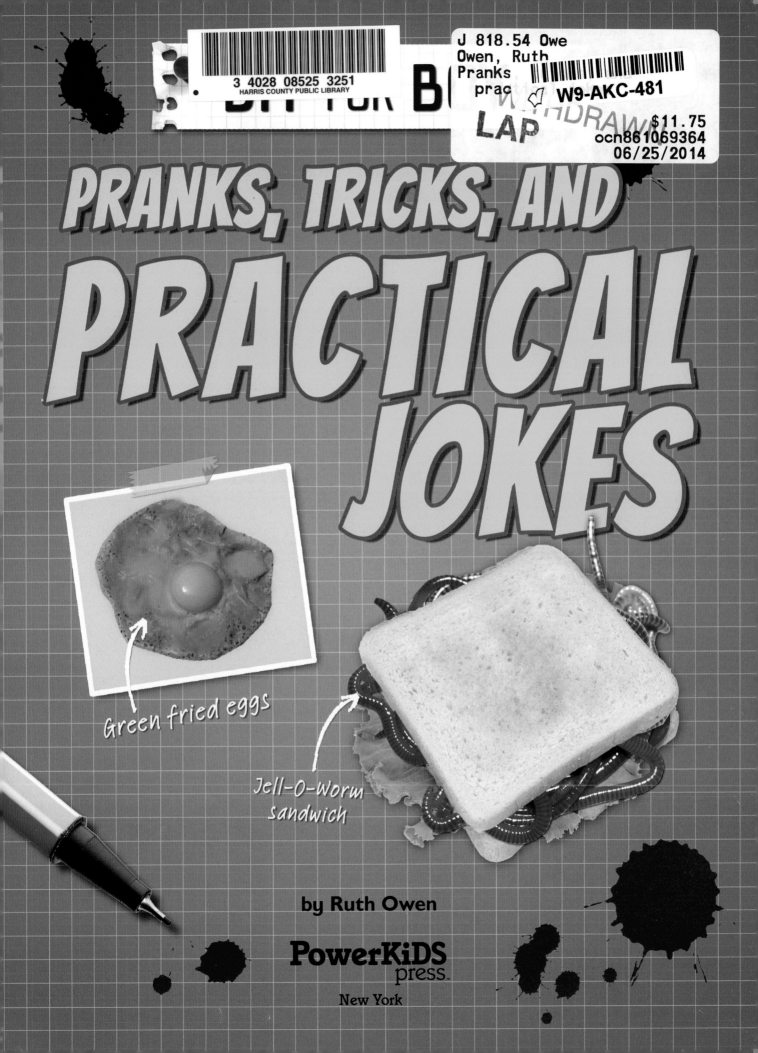

Green fried eggs

Jell-O-Worm sandwich

by Ruth Owen

PowerKiDS press.

New York

Published in 2014 by The Rosen Publishing Group, Inc.
29 East 21st Street, New York, NY 10010

Produced for Rosen by Ruby Tuesday Books Ltd
Editor for Ruby Tuesday Books Ltd: Mark J. Sachner
US Editor: Joshua Shadowens
Designer: Emma Randall

Photo Credits:
Cover, 1, 3, 5, 6-7, 8-9, 10-11, 13, 14-15, 16, 20-21 © Shutterstock; Cover, 1, 4-5, 6-7,
8-9, 10-11, 12, 14-15, 16-17, 18-19, 22-23, 24-25, 26-27, 28-29 © Ruby Tuesday
Books and John Such.

Publisher Cataloging Data

Owen, Ruth.
Pranks, tricks, and practical jokes / by Ruth Owen.
  p. cm. — (DIY for boys)
Includes index.
ISBN 978-1-4777-6294-3 (library binding) — ISBN 978-1-4777-6295-0 (pbk.) —
ISBN 978-1-4777-6296-7 (6-pack)
1. Tricks — Juvenile literature. 2. Practical jokes — Juvenile literature. I. Owen,
Ruth, 1967—. II. Title.
GV1548.O94 2014
793.8—d23

Manufactured in the United States of America

CPSIA Compliance Information: Batch #W14PK8 For Further Information contact: Rosen Publishing, New York, New York at 1-800-237-9932

CONTENTS

Gotcha! 4

The Worm Sandwich 6

The Never-Ending Thread 10

Torn Wallpaper Prank 12

Gruesome Green Eggs 14

Soda Explosion 18

Water Bottle Sprinkler 20

Mail with a Bang! 22

Bigfoot Was Here! 26

Glossary 30

Websites 31

Read More, Index 32

WARNING!

Neither the author nor the publisher shall be liable for any bodily harm or damage to property that may happen as a result of carrying out the practical jokes in this book.

GOTCHA!

An unsuspecting person is innocently going about his or her daily business. Then, suddenly, gotcha! He or she has become the **victim** of a **practical joke**. But what exactly is a practical joke?

A practical joke is usually played on one or more people, and the idea behind it is to confuse, embarrass, or surprise the victim. Victims of a practical joke are always let in on the joke in the end, however, and get to laugh at themselves along with the joker who played the trick.

These types of jokes are called "practical" because unlike a **verbal joke**, they involve equipment or **props** and need to be planned and set up in advance.

In this book, you will be getting practical creating props such as giant cardboard feet and green fried eggs. So get planning and making, and pull some cruel but cool practical jokes on your friends and family!

Worms are fascinating creatures that help make soil healthy. They eat dead plants and animals and then excrete out **nutrients** that living plants need as food.

Jell-O worms

All that wormy science stuff is cool. But what's also cool about worms is that they have the power to totally gross people out. And where there's the power to gross out, there's **potential** for a practical joke.

Make these Jell-O worms and hide them in a sandwich for a friend. Either let your friend bite into the sandwich, or just before he or she takes a bite, shout, "What's that wriggling in your sandwich?"

BAZINGA!

YOU WILL NEED:

- 100 flexible straws
- A tall container such as a juice carton
- A rubber band
- 10 ounces (280 g) of raspberry Jell-O
- 0.4 ounces (12 g) unflavored powdered gelatin
- A mixing bowl and spoon
- 2 pints (950 ml) boiling water
- 1 cup of whipping cream
- Green food coloring
- Bread and lettuce

STEP 1:

You will be using the straws as a mold to make the Jell-O worms, so begin by pulling, or flexing, out the straws to make the ridged part as long as possible.

STEP 2:

Place the straws into the container. You will need a tight fit to keep the straws upright. You can use a rubber band to keep them tightly together in a bundle.

STEP 3:

Place the Jell-O and unflavored gelatin in a bowl. Then add the boiling water and allow the Jell-O and gelatin to dissolve in the water.

STEP 4:

When the mixture is just warm, begin adding small quantities of the cream and just a few drops of green food coloring at a time. Stir thoroughly. Keep adding cream and food coloring until your worm mixture is the color you want it to be.

STEP 5:

Slowly pour the mixture into the straws. It's no problem if some mixture leaks out of the bottom of the straws into the container. Just keep filling the straws until the container is filled or all the mixture is gone

A tall glass also makes a good container for the straws.

STEP 6:

Leave the Jell-O worms to set in a refrigerator overnight.

STEP 7:
When the worm mixture is set firm, carefully remove the bundle of straws from the container and separate them.

STEP 8:
Starting at one end of a straw, use your fingers to gently squeeze the Jell-O worm from the straw.

STEP 9:
When your Jell-O worms are ready, make a worm and lettuce sandwich and get ready to gross out your friends!

THE NEVER-ENDING THREAD

This prank is super quick to set up, but it is a great way to play a trick on moms, aunts, grandmas, and just about anyone else who thinks it's their job to keep YOU looking neat!

YOU WILL NEED:
- A plain colored shirt or T-shirt
- A needle
- A long piece of white thread

STEP 1:
Thread the needle.

Leave 1 inch (2.5 cm) of thread

Thread pulled through

STEP 2:
Push the needle through the front of the shirt and pull the thread out through the neck hole. Leave about 1 inch (2.5 cm) of thread hanging on the front of the shirt.

STEP 3:

Take the needle off the thread. Carefully put on the shirt and then tuck the long piece of thread inside the shirt.

STEP 4:

When people spot a small loose thread on your shirt, they won't be able to resist trying to remove it. As the thread is pulled, however, instead of coming away from the shirt, it will get longer and longer and longer.

GOTCHA!

Something catching your eye, Mom?

TORN WALLPAPER PRANK

The torn wallpaper prank is an oldie, but a real goodie. It's entirely up to you how angry you allow the owner of the wallpaper to get before you let them in on the joke.

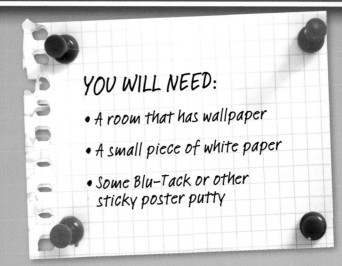

YOU WILL NEED:

• A room that has wallpaper

• A small piece of white paper

• Some Blu-Tack or other sticky poster putty

STEP 1:
Fold the piece of paper in half.

STEP 2:
Starting where the paper is creased, tear a diamond shape from the paper.

STEP 3:
Open up the diamond, turn it over, and attach small blobs of Blu-Tack to the top half.

STEP 4:

Now press the top half of the diamond onto a wall where there is wallpaper. Allow the bottom half to hang loose. The white paper will look just like a tear in the wallpaper.

STEP 5:

When the "tear" is discovered, take the blame, or deny all knowledge. See how long you can go without laughing!

13

GRUESOME GREEN EGGS

Cook up some green eggs for breakfast and horrify your friends or family! Using some red cabbage, you can turn the whites of eggs green.

Egg

How does it work? The colors in vegetables are made by materials called **pigments**. When the purplish-red pigment of red cabbage mixes with egg white, however, a chemical reaction takes place that turns the egg white green.

Cook a green egg and serve it to a friend. Or you can serve your friend a normal egg and give yourself a green egg. Then, as he or she watches in horror as you dig into your egg, say, "Oh, it's just a little moldy. I'm sure it will be fine!"

Red cabbage

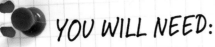

YOU WILL NEED:

- Red cabbage
- A knife and cutting board
- A saucepan
- Water
- Eggs
- Two small bowls (for separating the egg yolk from the egg white)

- A dessert spoon
- Cooking oil or butter
- A frying pan
- A spatula or egg turner
- A plate for serving

STEP 1:
Chop up half a cup of red cabbage.

WARNING!

Only use a stove if an adult is there to help you.

STEP 2:
Place the cabbage in the saucepan with two cups of water. Bring the water to a boil on the stove, then turn down the heat and cook the cabbage on a low heat for about 10 minutes. The water will turn purplish-red with juices from the cabbage.

STEP 3:
Allow the colored water to cool. You can keep it in the refrigerator for up to a week.

STEP 4:

Crack an egg by tapping it on the edge of a bowl. Separate the egg yolk from the white by gently prying apart the two halves of the shell and allowing the white to run from the shell into a bowl.

STEP 5:

Mix one dessert spoonful of cabbage water into the egg white. The egg white will immediately turn green!

Yolk

Egg white mixed with cabbage water

STEP 6:

To cook the egg, put a little oil or butter in the frying pan and put the pan onto the stove. Pour the egg white into the pan and start frying.

STEP 7:

Now pour the egg yolk onto the green egg white in the frying pan. Be very gentle so the yolk doesn't break. Fry the egg until fully cooked.

The green fried egg will look gruesome, but it is perfectly safe to eat and will taste just like a normal egg!

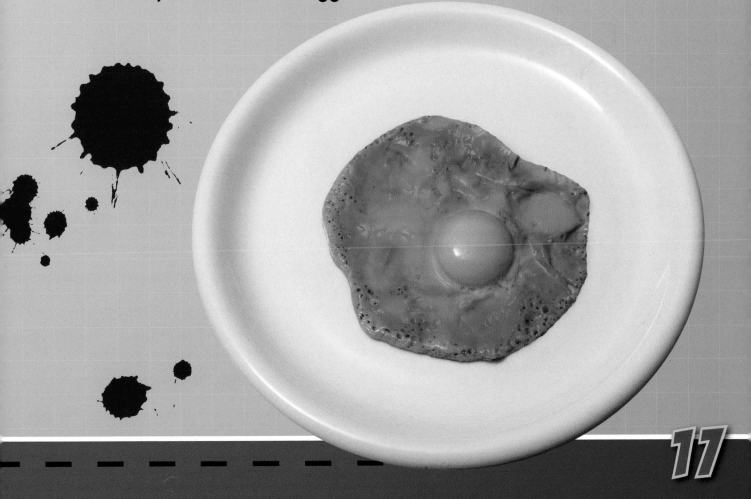

You may have seen what happens when you put Mentos mints into a bottle of soda. If you haven't, the soda explodes and erupts from the bottle! Here's a way to set up a soda bottle so that it explodes all over a friend when he or she least expects it. Make sure your friend isn't around anything that might get damaged!

YOU WILL NEED:
- A bottle of soda
- Mentos mints
- Thread and a large needle

STEP 1:
Thread the needle. Push the needle through a mint and pull the thread through.

STEP 2:
Tie a large knot in the end of the thread and then pull the thread through the mint up to the knot. Trim off any excess thread behind the knot.

STEP 3:

Open the cap of the soda and carefully dangle the mint in the neck of the bottle. Screw the cap back on so it tightens over the thread and holds the mint in place.

Trim off the thread here.

STEP 4:

Finally, cut the thread as close to the bottle cap as possible.

STEP 5:

When your friend unscrews the bottle cap, the mint will drop into the soda and begin fizzing. Within seconds, the soda will explode!

Try threading two or three mints together for a more powerful effect. Your friend probably won't notice the mints in the neck of the bottle because he or she won't be looking for them or expecting them to be there.

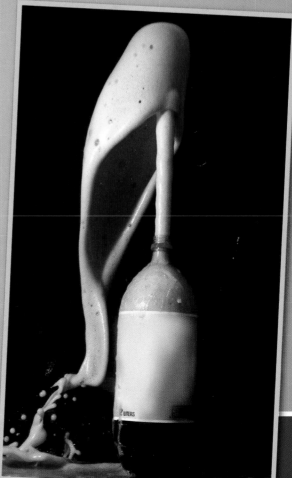

WATER BOTTLE SPRINKLER

Get your best friend soaking wet with this next prank. It takes just a minute or two to set up and will guarantee you a good laugh.

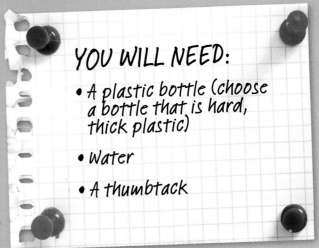

YOU WILL NEED:

- A plastic bottle (choose a bottle that is hard, thick plastic)
- Water
- A thumbtack

A thumbtack

Make the holes here.

STEP 1:

Fill the bottle with water so it is full to the very top. Screw on the cap tightly.

STEP 2:

Pierce several holes around the base of the bottle using a thumbtack. A little water will squirt from each hole as you pierce it, but then the water will stop flowing.

As long as the bottle's cap stays screwed shut, the water won't squirt out of the holes.

STEP 3:
Offer the bottle to a friend to drink from. As soon as he or she starts to unscrew the bottle's top, water will squirt from all the holes!

21

MAIL WITH A BANG!

This next practical joke shows you how to set up an envelope so it makes a loud bang as the **recipient** tries to remove the envelope's contents.

The bang will be made by the "banger" from a party popper. Be ready, though, for a very loud noise. When the banger is no longer surrounded by the contents of the party popper, the noise it makes is much louder than usual.

YOU WILL NEED:

- A large envelope
- A craft knife
- A party popper
- Scissors
- Two pieces of cardboard
- A stapler
- A hot glue gun
- A glue stick

WARNING:

Don't try out this joke on anyone who is easily scared or startled! Only use a glue gun if an adult is there to help you.

Unstick the envelope along the right-hand and bottom edges.

STEP 1:

Place the envelope face down. Using a craft knife, carefully unstick the envelope's right-hand edge and bottom edge.

Once the two edges are unstuck, open out the envelope.

Envelope opened out

STEP 2:
Cut open a party popper and remove the banger.

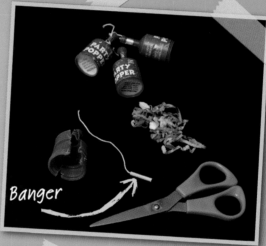

PARTY POPPER

PARTY POPPER

Banger

Half an inch (1 cm) border around the cardboard

STEP 3:
Cut the cardboard into two pieces. Each piece should be about half an inch (1 cm) narrower all the way round than the size of the envelope.

There should also be about a half an inch (1 cm) gap between the pieces of cardboard.

Half an inch (1 cm) gap

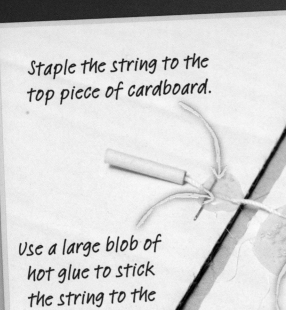

Staple the string to the top piece of cardboard.

Tie a knot in the banger's string.

Use a large blob of hot glue to stick the string to the cardboard, too.

Blob of hot glue

STEP 4:
Now attach the party popper banger to the two pieces of cardboard. It must be firmly fixed in place so that the string absolutely cannot move.

The top piece of cardboard should be loose.

Staple the string to the bottom piece of cardboard so that the knot cannot pull through the staple.

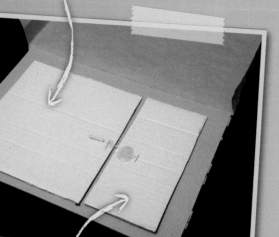

STEP 5:
Glue the bottom piece of cardboard to the envelope.

Reseal the back of the envelope.

The bottom piece of cardboard is glued in place.

STEP 6:
Using a glue stick, reseal the bottom and right-hand edges of the envelope.

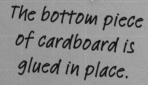

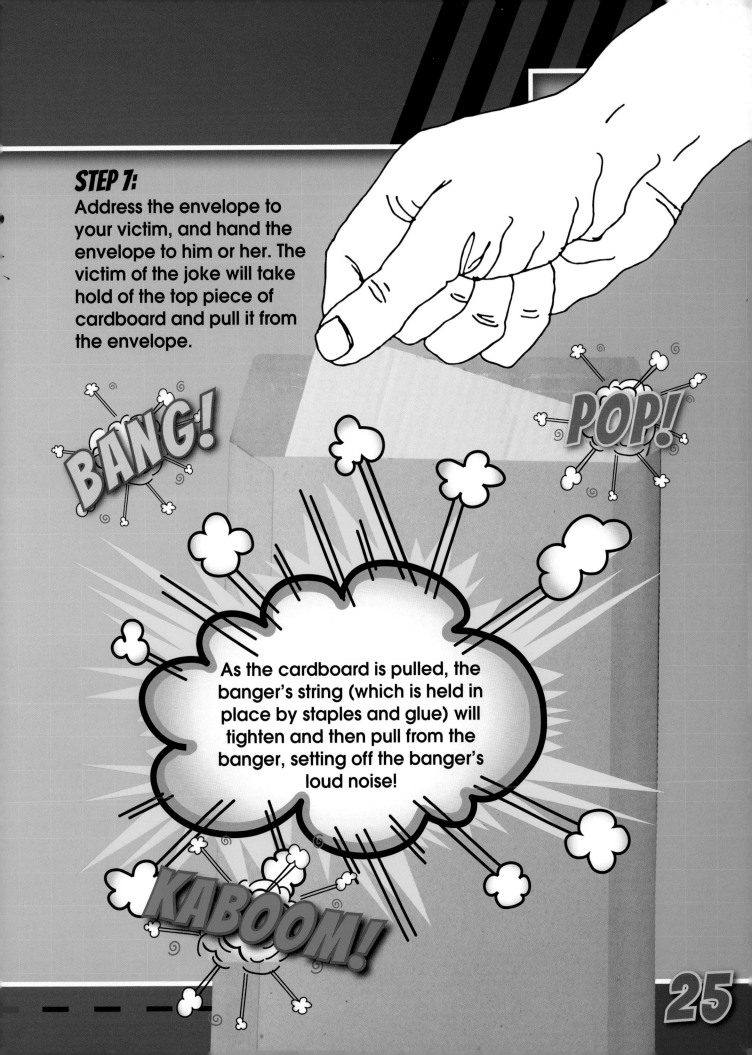

STEP 7:
Address the envelope to your victim, and hand the envelope to him or her. The victim of the joke will take hold of the top piece of cardboard and pull it from the envelope.

BANG!

POP!

As the cardboard is pulled, the banger's string (which is held in place by staples and glue) will tighten and then pull from the banger, setting off the banger's loud noise!

KABOOM!

For many years in North America, people have reported seeing huge, hairy, half-human, half-ape creatures. These giant, mysterious beasts are known as Bigfoots.

Eyewitnesses have reported sightings of 10-foot- (3-m-) tall Bigfoots. Footprints have even been found that are up to 27 inches (68.5 cm) long! Now, you can convince your neighbors that a Bigfoot is in town by creating fake **evidence** of a Bigfoot visit to your neighborhood. Build your own Bigfoot big feet, then make giant footprints in snow, soft mud, or sand where you can be sure a family member or neighbor will see them.

YOU WILL NEED:

- A large sheet of paper
- A pen
- Scissors
- Thick cardboard
- A craft knife
- A plank of wood and an adult to cut it into pieces
- A glue gun
- A pair of old sneakers
- Duct tape

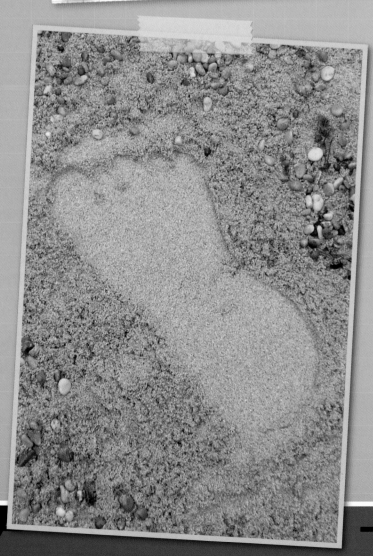

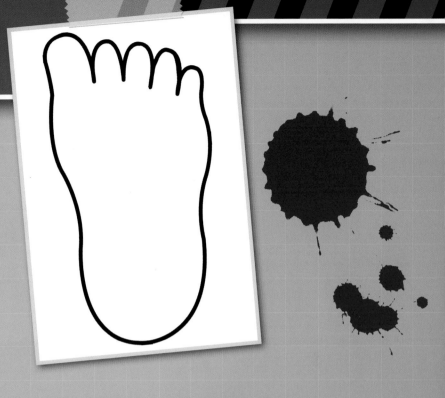

STEP 1:

Draw a template for your giant feet on the sheet of paper. Your big foot should be much bigger than a human foot. Cut out the paper template.

You only need to make one template because you can reverse it to make the second foot.

STEP 2:

Lay the paper template onto the cardboard and draw around it. Cut out the cardboard foot shape using the craft knife.

STEP 3:

Repeat Step 2 until you have three cardboard right feet and three left feet.

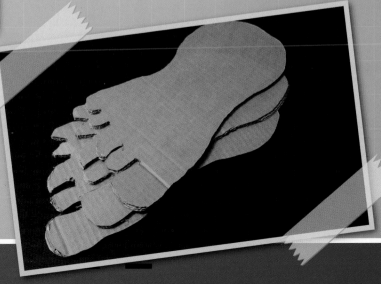

STEP 4:

Ask an adult to cut two pieces of wood that are slightly longer than your cardboard feet.

STEP 5:

Now put on the sneakers. While wearing the sneakers, tape them to the topside of each piece of wood using the duct tape.

Then wriggle your feet back out of the sneakers.

STEP 6:

Now tape a cardboard foot to the underside of each piece of wood.

This is the underside of a completed foot.

STEP 7:

Now glue the second and third cardboard foot shape to the underside of each piece of wood. The three layers of cardboard will make a deep impression in snow, soft mud, or sand.

The topside of the completed feet.

STEP 8:
Now put on your Bigfoot big feet and get busy making footprints.

When you've made some footprints, hide nearby to see people's reactions. Make sure you take photos of the Bigfoot prints as evidence of the creature's visit to your neighborhood.

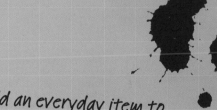

Add an everyday item to your photo to show the size of the footprint.

GLOSSARY

evidence (EH-vuh-dents)
Something that can prove or disprove a fact. For example, a footprint proves that a person or animal was in a particular place.

eyewitnesses (eye-WIT-nes-ez)
People who have personally seen something and are able to give a firsthand description of it.

nutrients (NOO-tree-ents)
Substances that living things need to grow, get energy, and stay healthy. For example, vitamins and protein are nutrients.

pigments (PIG-ments)
Substances that give other materials their colors.

potential (poh-TEN-shul)
The qualities or abilities that may be developed into something useful or successful in the future.

practical joke (PRAK-tih-kul JOHK)
A joke that involves practical work, such as making props, that are played on a victim to confuse, surprise, or embarrass that person.

props (PROPS)

Objects that are used in practical jokes, plays, movies, and TV shows. A prop might be a real object or a fake version, such as a fake bottle that is made from a material that looks like glass, but won't cut a person when it shatters.

recipient (ri-SIH-pee-unt)

A person who receives something, such as a piece of mail.

verbal joke (VER-bul JOHK)

A joke that is told, or spoken.

victim (VIK-tim)

The person to whom something happens.

WEBSITES

Due to the changing nature of Internet links, Powerkids Press has developed an online list of websites related to the subject of this book. This site is updated regularly. Please use this link to access the list: www.powerkidslinks.com/dfb/pranks/

READ MORE

Bell-Rehwoldt, Sheri. *The Kids' Guide to Pranks, Tricks, and Practical Jokes.* Kids' Guides. Mankato, MN: Capstone Press, 2009.

Churchhill, E. Richard. *Tricks and Pranks.* Little Giant Books. New York: Sterling, 2007.

Connolly, Sean and Kay Barnham. *The Funny Food Joke Book.* Laugh Out Loud. New York: Windmill Books, 2011.

INDEX

B
Bigfoot, 26

E
eggs, 4, 14–15, 16–17
envelopes, 22–23, 24–25

F
footprints, 26–27, 28–29

J
Jell-O, 6–7, 8–9

P
pigments, 14
practical jokes, 4, 6, 22

projects to make:
    Bigfoot was here!, 26–27, 28–29
    gruesome green eggs, 14–15, 16–17
    mail with a bang!, 22–23, 24–25
    never-ending thread, the, 10–11
    soda explosion, 18–19
    torn wallpaper prank, 12–13
    water bottle sprinkler, 20–21
    worm sandwich, the, 6–7, 8–9

props, 4

R
red cabbage, 14–15

S
soda, 18–19

T
thread, 10–11

V
verbal jokes, 4
victims of practical jokes, 4, 25

W
wallpaper, 12–13
water, 20–21
worms, 6